MW01264216

GREEK MYTHOLOGY

HEROES AND VILLAINS

by Maddie Spalding

BrightPoint Press

San Diego, CA

BrightPoint Press

© 2022 BrightPoint Press
an imprint of ReferencePoint Press, Inc.
Printed in the United States

For more information, contact:
BrightPoint Press
PO Box 27779
San Diego, CA 92198
www.BrightPointPress.com

LIBRARY OF CONGRESS CATALOGING-IN-PUBLICATION DATA

Names: Spalding, Maddie, author.
Title: Greek mythology heroes and villains / by Maddie Spalding.
Description: San Diego, CA : BrightPoint Press, [2022] | Series: The world of Greek
    mythology | Includes bibliographical references and index. | Audience: Grades 7-9
Identifiers: LCCN 2021040255 (print) | LCCN 2021040256 (eBook) | ISBN 9781678202583
    (hardcover) | ISBN 9781678202590 (eBook)
Subjects: LCSH: Heroes--Mythology--Juvenile literature. | Villains--Mythology--Juvenile
    literature. | Mythology, Greek--Juvenile literature.
Classification: LCC BL795.H46 S63 2022 (print) | LCC BL795.H46 (eBook) | DDC
    398.20938/02--dc23
LC record available at https://lccn.loc.gov/2021040255
LC eBook record available at https://lccn.loc.gov/2021040256

CONTENTS

AT A GLANCE

- Myths are the popular stories and beliefs shared by a culture. Greek writers first wrote down Greek myths between approximately 800 and 700 BCE.

- The ancient Greeks shared stories about heroes and villains. The villains tried to stop the heroes from succeeding.

- Many of the villains in Greek myths are kings. They make heroes go on difficult quests.

- Heracles is a well-known hero in Greek mythology. He completed many quests and became a god.

- Perseus is another hero in Greek mythology. He is known for killing a monster called Medusa.

- There are also famous heroic duos in Greek mythology. Medea helped Jason on his quest to get golden sheep fur, or fleece.

- Theseus and Ariadne are another heroic duo. Ariadne helped Theseus kill a monster and find his way out of a maze.

- Other heroes in Greek myths were warriors. Achilles and Odysseus fought in the Trojan War.

- Greek mythology continues to inspire people today. Many people have created works based on Greek myths, including movies and books.

HEROES AND VILLAINS IN GREEK MYTHS

Two snakes slithered up into a crib. A baby was inside. The baby's name was Heracles. The snakes showed their fangs. They prepared to strike and kill Heracles. But Heracles was not frightened. He grabbed the snakes. He choked them to death. Heracles had survived this threat.

Heracles is a famous Greek hero. His father was the king of the gods, Zeus.

However, he would face more danger in

the future.

Heracles was the son of Zeus and

Alcmene. Zeus was one of the gods.

Hera sent snakes to kill Heracles, but the baby defeated them.

Alcmene was a human. Zeus was married to the goddess Hera. Hera was angry at Zeus for having a son with another woman. Also, Zeus had said that Heracles would one day rule over Greece. Hera wanted to stop this from happening. She sent the snakes to kill Heracles. But her plan did not work. Heracles grew up to become a great warrior.

WHAT IS MYTHOLOGY?

Heracles is one of the most well-known heroes in Greek mythology. Mythology is a set of popular stories and beliefs shared by a culture. Individual stories are called myths.

Greek writers first recorded their myths

in writing between approximately 800 to

700 BCE.

Greek myths were connected to

religion. They described the gods many

ancient Greeks believed in. The myths also

included many other characters. Some,

like Heracles, were heroes. They went

on important journeys or missions. Other

characters were villains. They tried to stop

heroes from succeeding. But heroes often

succeeded anyway.

Sometimes the gods were the heroes

in Greek myths. The gods had many

Medusa was one villain Greek heroes faced. She had snakes for hair and could turn people to stone.

strengths. They were **immortal**. The gods

also controlled and influenced humans.

But the gods were not always heroic. In

some stories, they became the villains.

Unlike Greek gods, mortal Greek heroes were mortal and could die.

This happened when a hero made them angry. They would punish the hero.

Many heroes and villains in Greek myths were human. Humans in Greek myths were called **mortals**. Mortals had strengths and weaknesses. Writers described the mortal heroes as strong and brave. But, like the gods, these heroes sometimes got angry. They made bad decisions. Still, they did not give up in the face of danger. They succeeded against all odds.

CHAPTER ONE

HEROES ON QUESTS

Heroes in Greek mythology often went on quests. Quests are journeys or adventures. The heroes had special tasks to do. The quests were difficult. Villains often made heroes go on quests.

Heracles went on many quests. King Eurystheus gave Heracles these quests as punishment. The goddess Hera had cursed

Heracles visited Apollo's oracle at Apollo's temple in Delphi (pictured).

Heracles. She made him lose control of his actions and emotions. In a fit of madness, he killed his wife and children. Heracles was upset when he realized what he had done. He prayed to the god Apollo. Apollo's **oracle** told Heracles what he should do.

Oracles in Greek myths spoke directly with the gods. They shared the gods' messages with humans. The oracle gave Heracles instructions. Heracles would have to serve King Eurystheus for twelve years.

HERACLES'S QUESTS

King Eurystheus was a villain in Greek mythology. He made Heracles go on difficult quests. For example, Heracles had to kill a hydra. The hydra was a monster. It was a giant, poisonous snake with nine heads. It lived in a swamp. One of its heads was immortal. This head was said to be indestructible.

Heracles took his nephew Iolaus with him on this quest. Iolaus was a mortal and a friend to Heracles. Heracles was supposed to complete the quests on his own. Iolaus's job was to steer Heracles's **chariot**. Then he was supposed to leave Heracles alone to complete the quest.

HERACLES OR HERCULES?

In ancient times, there were more stories and art about Heracles than any other hero. Many Greeks worshipped him. Heracles's name means "glorious gift of Hera." Heracles's mother named him this to honor Hera. In the Greek myths, he was known as *Heracles* or *Herakles*. The Romans called him *Hercules*. Today, he is more commonly known by his Roman name.

King Eurystheus demanded that Heracles kill a hydra.

Heracles attacked the hydra's heads with his club. He smashed one head. Then, two more heads grew in its place. Also, a large crab started to bite Heracles's foot.

Heracles was in trouble. He called out for Iolaus. Iolaus came to help. He carried a torch. He put the flames on the hydra's necks. This kept new heads from growing. Finally, Heracles destroyed all the hydra's heads. He cut off the hydra's immortal head. He buried the head and covered the spot with a heavy rock. He did this so the head would not come back to life.

King Eurystheus heard of Heracles's victory. But he was not impressed. He told Heracles that this victory did not count. Iolaus had helped him. The king made Heracles complete ten more quests.

JOURNEYING TO THE UNDERWORLD

Heracles's final quest was the most challenging of all. Heracles had to kidnap Cerberus. Cerberus was a beast. The Greek writer Apollodorus, who lived in about 100 BCE, described Cerberus. He said the beast had three dog heads, "the tail of a dragon, and on his back the heads of all sorts of snakes."[1]

Cerberus guarded a river in the underworld. The underworld was a place deep underground. The souls of dead people lived there. The god Hades ruled over the underworld. Heracles had no

Cerberus was an intimidating three-headed beast. He lived in the underworld.

help on this last task. He wrestled and

kidnapped Cerberus on his own. He

brought Cerberus to King Eurystheus.

Heracles had completed all the king's

tasks. He was recognized as a hero.

He also gained something even more

important and rare. The god Apollo had made a promise to Heracles. Heracles would become a god if he completed all the quests. This meant that Heracles became immortal.

PERSEUS AND MEDUSA

Perseus is another hero in Greek mythology. The villain in Perseus's story was Polydectes. Polydectes was the king of the island of Serifos. He wanted to marry Perseus's mother. Perseus was against this. The king agreed not to marry Perseus's mother on one condition. He demanded Perseus kill a monster. The monster was called Medusa. She had snakes for hair.

Her gaze turned people into stone.

Hermes and Athena helped Perseus

defeat Medusa. Hermes was a god and a

messenger. He carried messages from the

gods. He also protected people on their

travels. Hermes gave Perseus a sword

ZEUS'S CHILDREN

Perseus was related to Heracles. Perseus was
the grandfather of Heracles's mother. He was
also Heracles's brother. Zeus was the father
of both men. Zeus had children with many
women. Some of Zeus's children were gods.
Athena and Hermes were Zeus's children. They
often helped heroes complete quests. Some
of Zeus's other children were mortals. Many of
them were heroes in Greek myths.

Perseus defeated the villain Medusa.

and shield. The shield belonged to the

goddess Athena.

Perseus did not look directly at Medusa.

Instead, he looked at her reflection in his

shield. This prevented him from turning

into stone. Perseus cut off Medusa's head.

He carried the head with him on his journey back to Serifos. Along the way, Perseus saved a woman from a sea monster. The woman's name was Andromeda. She was stranded on a rock in the middle of the sea. Perseus showed Medusa's head to the sea monster. Medusa's gaze turned the monster to stone.

Perseus married Andromeda after saving her. Then, he returned to Serifos. He showed Medusa's head to Polydectes. The king turned into stone. Perseus had defeated his enemies. But this was not the end of his story. Perseus later accidentally

The gates to Perseus's city Mycenae featured two lions.

killed his grandfather. They were both

participating in athletic games. Perseus

threw a heavy disc. The disc struck and

killed Perseus's grandfather. Perseus was

upset and ashamed. He left his home,

Argos, behind. He then founded his own

city called Mycenae.

THE QUALITIES OF A HERO

Both Perseus and Heracles were given tasks that seemed impossible. Still, they succeeded. Their strength and bravery helped them succeed. They overcame challenges and defeated villains.

Professor Seth Jeppesen studies Greek mythology. He explains how these Greek heroes are like today's superheroes. He says they both have "a special skill or quality . . . that makes them stand out."[2] But they also have flaws. They make mistakes. They often cannot complete quests on their own. They need help from others.

CHAPTER TWO

HEROIC DUOS

The main heroes in Greek myths were men. But female heroes often helped them succeed. Jason and Medea were a famous pair in Greek mythology. So were Theseus and Ariadne. Jason and Theseus completed difficult quests. Medea helped Jason. Ariadne helped Theseus. The men would not have been able to complete their quests without help from these women.

Ariadne (pictured) helped the hero Theseus on his quests.

JASON'S QUEST

Jason was the son of the king of Iolcus. He should have become king when his father died. But Jason's half uncle Pelias took the throne instead. Pelias did not want Jason to become king. So he sent Jason on a quest.

Jason had to journey to Colchis. There was

a special sheep in Colchis. It had golden fur,

or fleece. Jason had to bring this fleece to

Pelias. If he succeeded, Pelias promised he

would allow Jason to become king. Pelias

thought this quest was impossible. He did

not think Jason would survive it.

WHO WERE THE ARGONAUTS?

The *Argo* was named after its builder, Argus.
The ancient Greek word *naut* means "voyager."
Argus was one of the Argonauts. Heracles
also joined the crew for part of their journey.
Orpheus was another crewmember. He was a
musician and poet. All of the Argonauts were
heroes. They had special skills. For example,
Orpheus could charm animals with his music.

Jason sailed to Colchis on a ship called the *Argo*. He had a crew of fifty men. They called themselves the Argonauts. Apollonius was an ancient Greek writer. He described the day the Argonauts left for Colchis. On that day, "the gods looked down from heaven upon the ship and the might of the heroes."[3]

The Argonauts encountered many obstacles on their journey. For example, they had to sail past moving cliffs. Some of the Argonauts died. But Jason survived.

The Argonauts finally arrived at Colchis. King Aeëtes ruled over Colchis. He owned

The Greek city of Volos recreated Jason's ship, the Argo.

the golden fleece. He gave Jason a few

difficult tasks to do. He asked Jason to

complete these tasks in one day. If he did,

the king promised to give him the fleece.

MEDEA HELPS JASON

Medea was King Aeëtes's daughter. The

god Eros struck Medea with one of his

arrows. Eros's arrows made people fall in love. Medea fell in love with Jason. Apollonius described this scene in *The Argonautica*. When the arrow hit Medea, "her soul melted with the sweet pain."[4] Jason told Medea he loved her too. He promised to marry her after he got the golden fleece.

Jason's first task involved two fire-breathing bulls. Jason had to use these bulls to plow a field. Then, he needed to plant dragon teeth in the field. Medea gave Jason a potion. Jason rubbed this potion on himself. It protected him from the bulls' fire.

Jason tamed the bulls and plowed the field. Then, he tossed the dragon teeth onto the field. Soldiers grew up from the ground. Medea had warned Jason this would happen. She told him how to stop the soldiers from attacking him. Jason threw a rock in between the soldiers. The soldiers did not know Jason had thrown the rock. They started fighting and killing each other.

Jason successfully completed King Aeëtes's tasks. But the king did not give up his fleece. He threatened to kill the Argonauts. Despite these threats, Medea continued to help Jason. She led Jason

Jason snatched the fleece after Medea put the dragon to sleep.

to an oak tree. The fleece hung from the

tree. A dragon guarded the fleece. Medea

fed the dragon a potion. The potion

put the dragon to sleep. Then Jason

stole the fleece. Medea, Jason, and the Argonauts fled Colchis with the fleece.

Jason and the Argonauts arrived back in Iolcus. Jason gave the fleece to King Pelias. But the king still would not give up his throne. Medea tried to help Jason. She came up with a trick to kill the king. She killed an old sheep. She put the sheep's meat into a pot with magical herbs. A young lamb emerged from the pot. She showed Pelias's daughters her magical skills. They wanted to try this spell on Pelias to make him young again. They killed their father and cut him up. But Medea did not add the

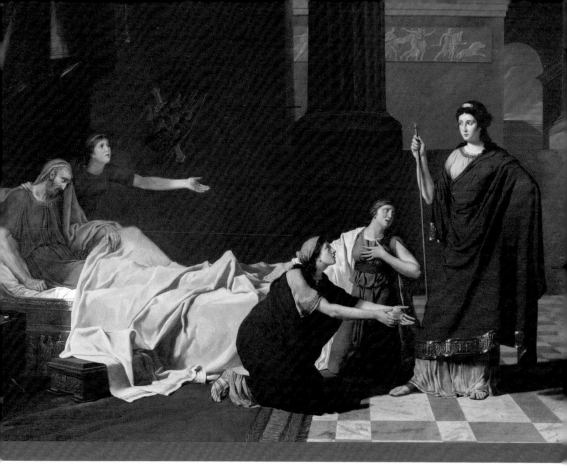

Medea (right) tricked Pelias's daughters into killing their father.

magical herbs to the pot. The spell did not

work. The women had killed their father.

Pelias's son took over as king instead

of Jason. The son made Jason and

Medea leave Iolcus. They settled in the

city of Corinth. Jason abandoned Medea. Many years later, Jason finally became king of Iolcus.

THESEUS AND ARIADNE

Theseus and Ariadne were another heroic duo in Greek mythology. Ariadne was the daughter of King Minos. King Minos ruled over a Greek island called Crete. The king sent his only son to Athens to kill a bull. But the bull killed the king's son. King Minos was angry and upset. He ordered his troops to invade Athens.

Then, he punished the people of Athens. He demanded the Athenians send seven

King Minos's daughter Ariadne helped Theseus with his quests.

young men and seven young women

to Crete each year. There was a maze

underneath Minos's palace in Crete. A

Minotaur was inside the maze. This creature

was half bull and half human. King Minos

forced the men and women to enter the

maze. The Minotaur ate them all.

Theseus wanted to put an end to

these killings. He was the son of the king

of Athens. He volunteered to be sent

ARIADNE'S FATE

Theseus returned to Athens after killing the Minotaur. Ariadne came with him on this journey. What happened to Ariadne next is unclear. Some Greek writers wrote that Theseus abandoned her on an island. Others wrote that a god made Theseus leave her on the island. This god was Dionysus. He was the god of wine. In all of the versions of this myth, Dionysus and Ariadne married. They had children.

into the maze one year. He hoped to kill the Minotaur.

Ariadne fell in love with Theseus. She decided to help him. She gave him a ball of thread. Theseus unspooled the thread as he went through the maze. The thread would help him find his way out.

In some versions of this story, Theseus killed the beast by pounding it with his fists. In other versions, Ariadne gave Theseus a sword. He used the sword to kill the Minotaur. A female hero had helped a male hero save the day.

CHAPTER THREE

HEROES AND VILLAINS AT WAR

Wars and battles happened often in Greek mythology. Several heroes in Greek myths were warriors. The Trojan War was one famous war. Many Greek heroes fought in it. The Greeks fought against the Trojans in this war. The Trojans lived in a city called Troy.

The ruins of the ancient city of Troy can be seen in modern-day Turkey.

WHAT WAS THE TROJAN WAR?

The Trojan War started with a kidnapping.

A man named Paris kidnapped a woman

named Helen. Helen was a Greek woman.

Paris was the son of Priam, the king of Troy. Paris took Helen back with him to Troy.

Helen was married to King Menelaus. King Menelaus ruled over the Greek city of Sparta. He was upset to learn Paris had taken Helen. He wanted his wife back. Menelaus's brother, Agamemnon, organized an army. Agamemnon was the king of Mycenae. The Greek army planned to invade Troy and bring Helen back.

The Greek poet Homer wrote about the Trojan War in 700 BCE. His poem about the war was called the *Iliad*. Homer described the gathering of the Greek army. He wrote

IMPORTANT EVENTS IN ANCIENT GREECE

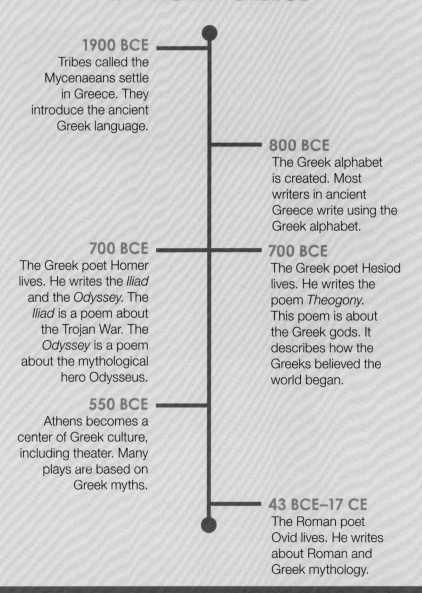

1900 BCE
Tribes called the Mycenaeans settle in Greece. They introduce the ancient Greek language.

800 BCE
The Greek alphabet is created. Most writers in ancient Greece write using the Greek alphabet.

700 BCE
The Greek poet Homer lives. He writes the *Iliad* and the *Odyssey*. The *Iliad* is a poem about the Trojan War. The *Odyssey* is a poem about the mythological hero Odysseus.

700 BCE
The Greek poet Hesiod lives. He writes the poem *Theogony*. This poem is about the Greek gods. It describes how the Greeks believed the world began.

550 BCE
Athens becomes a center of Greek culture, including theater. Many plays are based on Greek myths.

43 BCE–17 CE
The Roman poet Ovid lives. He writes about Roman and Greek mythology.

The history of ancient Greece spans more than 1,000 years.

Greek king Peleus (left) was Achilles's father.

there were as many men "as the leaves and flowers produced by spring."[5] Many of these soldiers were heroes in Greek mythology. Achilles was one of the most famous heroes.

THE HERO ACHILLES

Achilles was the son of Peleus, a mortal Greek king. Achilles's mother, Thetis, was a nymph. Nymphs were minor goddesses. They controlled and shaped parts of nature, such as rivers and trees. Although they were goddesses, they did not live forever. But they did live for a long time.

When Achilles was a child, Thetis heard a **prophecy** about him. A prophecy is a prediction. The prophecy said Achilles would become a hero. However, he would also die young. Thetis wanted to prevent this from happening. She brought Achilles to the River Styx in the underworld.

This river had protective powers. The river water protected mortals from harm. Thetis dipped Achilles in the river. But she missed one part of his body. This part was his heel, where Thetis had held him. Achilles's heel was his weakness. It was the only part of his body that could be harmed.

Achilles later fought in the Trojan War. The war lasted ten years. Along the way to Troy, Achilles and his crew had stopped at the island of Tenedos. Fighters on the island attacked Achilles and his men. Tenes was the king of Tenedos. He was also Apollo's son. Achilles killed Tenes. Apollo was angry.

He vowed to take revenge on Achilles.

Achilles was a fierce warrior and leader.

But he withdrew from the fighting in Troy

at one point. He had a disagreement

with Agamemnon. He refused to fight

for the Greek army. He asked his friend,

ACHILLES'S HEEL

Today, *Achilles's heel* is a popular phrase. It refers to a person's weakness. For example, pride or anger could be someone's Achilles's heel. These traits could cause problems in the person's life. There is also a part of the body called the Achilles tendon. This is a band of tissue inside the body. It connects the heel bone to the calf muscles. Achilles tendon injuries can take a long time to heal.

Patroclus, to fight in his place. Patroclus wore Achilles's armor in battle. The Trojan hero Hector mistook Patroclus for Achilles. Hector killed Patroclus.

Achilles was upset when he heard Hector had killed Patroclus. Achilles rejoined the fighting. He wanted to avenge his friend's death. Achilles killed Hector in battle. He also led the Greeks to victory in other battles.

ACHILLES'S FATE

However, Achilles did not survive the war. The villain in Achilles's story was Apollo. Apollo held a grudge against Achilles.

Paris's arrow mortally wounded Achilles in his heel.

He was still angry that Achilles had killed his son.

Paris was upset when he learned Achilles had killed Hector. Hector was Paris's brother. Apollo told Paris that Achilles would try to sneak into Troy. Paris shot an arrow at Achilles as Achilles entered the city. Apollo guided the arrow. The arrow hit Achilles's

heel. Achilles died. Though he did not have

a long life, Achilles became one of the most

well-known heroes of Greek mythology.

ODYSSEUS'S INVENTION

Odysseus was another Greek hero who

fought in the Trojan War. He was the king of

Ithaca. Ithaca is an island in Greece.

The Greek writer Hesiod described

Odysseus as "patient-minded."[6] Odysseus

was smart and brave. He came up with

an idea that helped the Greeks win the

war. He told the Greek troops to build a

giant wooden horse. The horse was hollow

inside. Some Greek soldiers hid inside it. The Greek troops pretended to retreat and surrender. A Greek soldier left the horse outside the gates of Troy. He told the Trojans it was a gift for Athena. This was a lie. It was all part of Odysseus's plan.

The Trojans believed the lie. They brought the horse into Troy. The Greek

THE POET HOMER

The Greek poet Homer wrote the *Odyssey* around 700 BCE. This poem tells the story of Odysseus's journey home from the Trojan War. The Greeks viewed Homer as the greatest writer of their time. Homer also wrote the *Iliad*. He wrote this poem before the *Odyssey*. Odysseus is mentioned in this poem too.

soldiers snuck out of the horse at night. They opened the city gates. The rest of the Greek army was waiting outside. The army invaded the city. The Greeks defeated the Trojans and found Helen. The war was finally over.

ODYSSEUS'S JOURNEY HOME

Odysseus had not wanted to fight in the Trojan War. He was eager to return home after the war ended. He wanted to reunite with his wife, Penelope, and their son.

The main villain in Odysseus's story was the god Poseidon. Poseidon was the god of the sea. Odysseus and his crew came

Odysseus and his crew faced the Cyclops Polyphemus on their ten-year journey home.

across a Cyclops on their journey back

to Ithaca. In Greek mythology, a Cyclops

was a one-eyed giant. This Cyclops's

name was Polyphemus. He was one of

Poseidon's sons. Polyphemus ate some

of Odysseus's crew. Odysseus stabbed

Polyphemus's eye with a spike and blinded

him. Then Odysseus and his men escaped.

Polyphemus was angry. He asked Poseidon to delay Odysseus's journey home.

Odysseus's journey back to Ithaca took ten years. Odysseus and his crew faced many obstacles. One obstacle they encountered was the monster Scylla. Scylla lived inside a cave in the sea. She had six heads with long, snakelike necks. She had many sharp teeth. Odysseus and his crew had to pass by Scylla. Scylla's heads seized six of Odysseus's men. But Odysseus survived.

Odysseus finally made it back to Ithaca. In his absence, many men had tried to

Odysseus killed Penelope's suitors when he returned home to Ithaca.

marry Penelope. They were gathered at Odysseus's palace. Odysseus was sometimes violent. He killed all of these men. He reunited with his wife and son. Like other heroes in Greek myths, Odysseus had achieved his goal against all odds.

CHAPTER FOUR

THE LEGACY OF GREEK HEROES AND VILLAINS

Greek myths were written thousands of years ago. Yet they have continually inspired people throughout history. Music, plays, operas, and artwork feature Greek myths. Many modern movies and books are based on these stories too.

*Greek myths inspired English playwright
William Shakespeare.*

GREEK HEROES AND VILLAINS IN THE ARTS

Greek myths have a lot of drama and action. They contain messages and **themes** such as loyalty and honor. These stories have long entertained audiences and readers.

Writers such as William Shakespeare have used Greek myths for inspiration. Shakespeare was an English playwright. He wrote the play *Troilus and Cressida* in the early 1600s. Troilus and Cressida were both Trojans. Troilus was one of King Priam's sons. Cressida was the daughter of a man named Calchas. Calchas joined the Greek

forces and betrayed the Trojans. Troilus

and Cressida fell in love. Then, Calchas

demanded to be reunited with his daughter.

Cressida was sent to Greece against

her will. She fell in love with another man

THE *ODYSSEUS* SYMPHONY

Alan Hovhaness was a composer. He wrote symphonies, or music for orchestras. In 1973, he wrote a symphony inspired by the story of Odysseus. It was called the *Odysseus* Symphony. Some parts of the symphony sound loud and frightening. These parts show the dangers Odysseus faced on his journey home. Another part of the symphony sounds like a soft love song. This part portrays the moment Odysseus and Penelope reunite.

Troilus and Cressida fell in love before Cressida's father sent her to Greece.

in Greece. *Troilus and Cressida* is a story of heartbreak and loss. Troilus lost Cressida. He also lost his brother Hector. One scene in the play depicts Achilles killing Hector. Other Greek heroes such as Odysseus also appear in the play.

Greek myths have also inspired musical composers. One composer was Gabriel Fauré. Fauré wrote an opera called *Pénélope* in the early 1900s. Musicians first performed this opera in 1913. The main character in this opera is Odysseus's wife, Penelope. The opera explores her experiences as she waits for Odysseus to return home. The opera shows how Penelope is reunited with Odysseus after twenty years.

MOVIES BASED ON GREEK MYTHS

Many modern films portray Greek myths. Heracles's story has been made into films

The Trojan horse from the movie Troy was gifted to the Turkish town of Canakkale.

for kids and adults. Some of these films are only loosely based on his story. Some parts of the Heracles myth are not kid friendly. For example, Disney released the animated movie *Hercules* in 1997. It includes a few of Heracles's quests. In the movie, Heracles falls in love with a woman named Megara. In the myth, Megara was Heracles's first wife. Heracles later kills Megara and their children. This detail is not included in the movie *Hercules*. Also, the main villain in the movie is Hades, not King Eurystheus.

Other filmmakers have also been inspired by Greek heroes. In 2004, the movie *Troy* came out. It was based on the myth of

the Trojan War. Achilles and Odysseus are

important characters in the movie. In 2010,

the movie *Clash of the Titans* was released.

Perseus is the main character in this movie.

The movie tells the story of Perseus,

including his killing of Medusa.

MODERN BOOKS BASED ON GREEK MYTHS

Several modern authors have adapted

Greek myths into popular books. Author

Rick Riordan wrote a series of children's

books. This series is called Percy Jackson

and the Olympians. Riordan created many

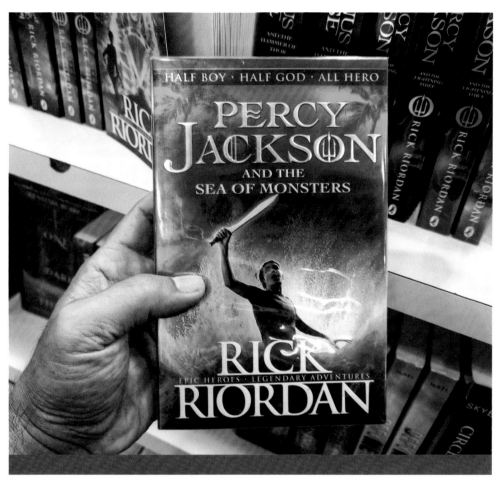

The Sea of Monsters *is the second novel in the Percy Jackson series.*

new characters. But he based his stories

on Greek myths. *The Lightning Thief* is the

first book in the series. Percy Jackson is the

main character. In the book, Percy learns he

is a demigod. One of his parents is mortal and the other is a god. Percy's father is Poseidon. His mother is a mortal. Percy meets other demigods. They fight monsters and go on quests.

The other books in the series feature Greek heroes. Percy's journey in *The Sea of Monsters* is similar to Odysseus's journey. Like the Greek hero Jason, Percy searches for the golden fleece. He faces the obstacles and monsters Odysseus also faced. The final Percy Jackson book, *The Last Olympian*, is based on the Trojan War. It mentions Achilles.

The Percy Jackson series became widely popular. It introduced Greek myths to new audiences. The first two books in the series were made into movies.

EXPLORING FEMALE STORIES

Jennifer Saint wanted to write a different version of a Greek myth. Saint noticed most female characters had small roles in the stories. Saint says, "The themes that stood out to me . . . were women being overlooked."[7] Saint's book *Ariadne* was published in 2021. It tells the story of how Ariadne helped Theseus defeat the Minotaur. Saint wrote the story from Ariadne's perspective. She also added background about Ariadne's life. Saint has made Greek **heroines** as interesting as Greek heroes.

Odysseus met Circe (middle) on his journey home to Ithaca.

Women were typically villains or minor characters in Greek myths. But in some books inspired by Greek myths, the women are the main characters. Madeline Miller wrote the book *Circe* in 2018. The book is about a female character named Circe. Odysseus meets Circe on his journey. Circe is a nymph who has magical powers. In Homer's poem the *Odyssey*, Circe turns some of Odysseus's men into pigs. Circe also distracts Odysseus. Odysseus forgets about his goal to return home. In *Circe*, Miller provides backstory for the character Circe. Miller writes the story from Circe's perspective.

WHY DO PEOPLE LIKE GREEK MYTHS?

The characters in Greek myths are imperfect. Both heroes and villains make mistakes. They struggle with human

Thousands of years after the ancient Greeks built their temples and told their stories, their mythology remains popular.

emotions such as anger and jealousy. This makes them relatable to audiences.

Miller explains how these factors help Greek myths stay popular. She says, "Culture has changed, but human beings and the things that we struggle with . . . are all still with us."[8] Some popular stories have been forgotten over time. But even after thousands of years, people continue to be drawn to Greek myths.

GLOSSARY

chariot

a carriage pulled by horses

heroines

female heroes

immortal

unable to die

mortals

people who do not live forever

oracle

a person in Greek mythology who communicates with the gods and shares the gods' messages with mortals

prophecy

a prediction that someone called a seer makes

themes

the main subjects or issues explored in a particular work, such as a book

SOURCE NOTES

CHAPTER ONE: HEROES ON QUESTS

1. James George Frazer, *Apollodorus: The Library*. New York: GP Putnam's Sons, 1921. p. 233.

2. Quoted in Sam Bigelow, "Modern and Ancient Heroes Share Common Themes, BYU Professors Say," *Daily Universe*, August 18, 2017. https://universe.byu.edu.

CHAPTER TWO: HEROIC DUOS

3. RC Seaton, *Apollonius Rhodis: The Argonautica*. Cambridge, MA: Harvard University Press, 1912.

4. RC Seaton, *Apollonius Rhodis: The Argonautica*.

CHAPTER THREE: HEROES AND VILLAINS AT WAR

5. George Chapman, *The Iliads of Homer, Prince of Poets, Never Before in Any Language Truly Translated, with a Comment upon Some of His Chief Places*. Vol. 1. London: Charles Knight and Company, 1843. p. 16.

6. Hesiod. *Theogony & Works and Days*. Translated by Stephanie Nelson and Richard Caldwell. Indianapolis, IN: Hackett, 2015. p. 62.

CHAPTER FOUR: THE LEGACY OF GREEK HEROES AND VILLAINS

7. Quoted in Kelly Maquire, "Interview: Ariadne by Jennifer Saint," *World History Encyclopedia*, May 26, 2021. www.worldhistory.org.

8. Quoted in Ezra Klein, "Madeline Miller on Myth, Nostalgia, and How Power Corrupts," *Vox*, April 24, 2020. www.vox.com.

FOR FURTHER RESEARCH

BOOKS

Eric Braun, *Greek Myths*. Minneapolis, MN: Capstone, 2019.

A. W. Buckey, *Greek Gods, Heroes, and Mythology*. Minneapolis, MN: Abdo, 2019.

Sara Green, *Ancient Greece*. Minneapolis, MN: Bellwether, 2020.

INTERNET SOURCES

"5 Terrifying Tales from Greek Mythology," *National Geographic Kids*, 2021. www.natgeokids.com.

"Who Were the Ancient Greek Gods and Heroes?" *BBC*, 2021. www.bbc.co.uk.

"Who Were the Ancient Greeks?" *BBC*, 2021. www.bbc.co.uk.

WEBSITES

Greek Myths
American Museum of Natural History
www.amnh.org/exhibitions/mythic-creatures/air/greek-myths

Discover more famous heroes, monsters, and creatures from
Greek myths.

Homer and the Gods
PBS Learning Media
https://tpt.pbslearningmedia.org/resource/thegreeks_ep2_
clip01/thegreeks_ep2_clip01/

Learn about Homer and the origins of Greek myths.

Myths and Heroes
PBS
www.pbs.org/mythsandheroes/myths_what.html

This website explains what myths are and the purpose of myths.

INDEX

IMAGE CREDITS

ABOUT THE AUTHOR

Maddie Spalding enjoys learning about history and cultures. She studied Greek mythology and the Greek language in college. She has written more than fifty children's books on a variety of topics. She lives in Minneapolis, Minnesota, with her husband and their dog.